THIS BOOK BELONGS TO

Dear Halloween lover,

On behalf of BRAINYINK, we would like to thank you for buying this Halloween Quotes Coloring Book. We value the trust you have put in our Halloween coloring book for all family members, and would like to thank you for that. BRAINYINK is always pleased to serving you and we certainly look forward to making more interesting fun books.

*Your **feedback** is very important as we are constantly looking for ways to improve our books' quality and get who ever owns this book the best experience ever.*

Thank you very much

COLOR TEST PAGE

THIS BOOK IS MADE WITH LOVE AND IT IS DEDICATED TO ALL AMAZING PEOPLE CELEBRATING THE HALLOWEEN

Copyright © 2020 by BRAINYINK

HAPPY HAUNTING!

EAT, DRINK
AND BE
SCARY!

HAPPY HAUNTING!

EAT, DRINK AND BE SCARY!

WHAT'S UP,
PUMPKIN?

STOP IN FOR
A SPELL

I WITCH YOU
A HAPPY
HALLOWEEN

PLEASE PARK
ALL BROOMS
AT THE DOOR

CAUTION!
WITCH
CROSSING

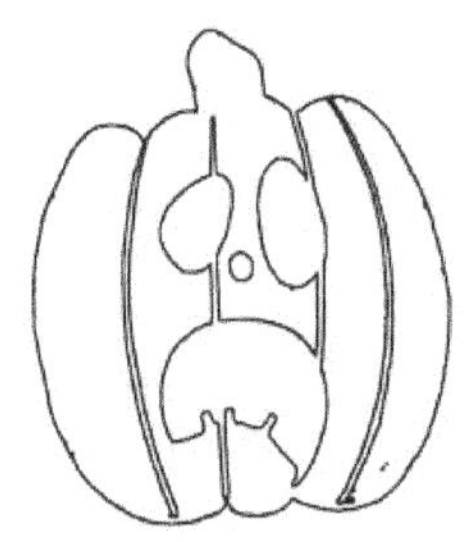

BOO TO YOU FROM OUR CREW

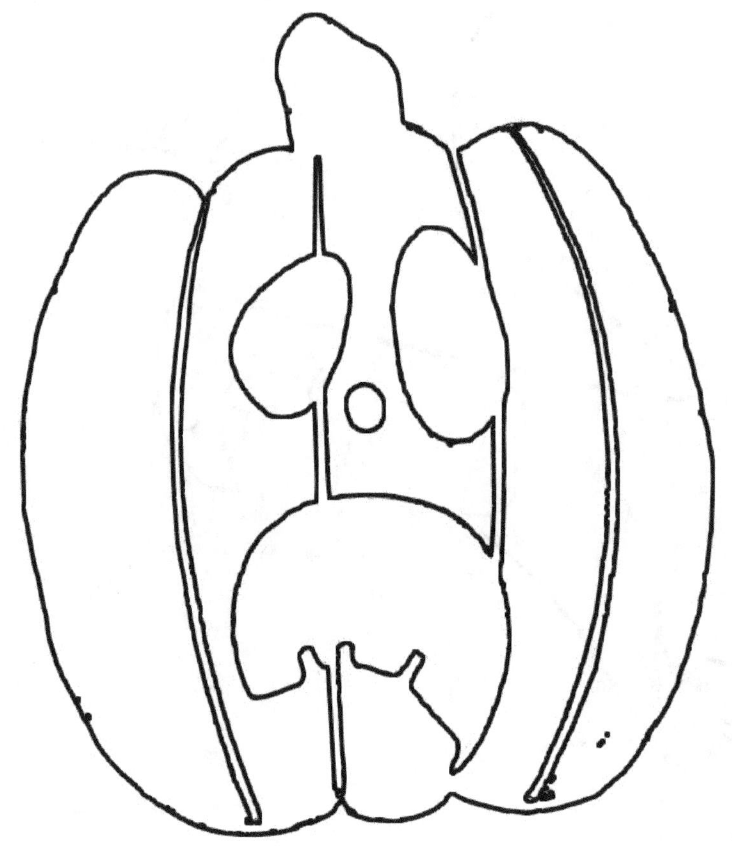

GHOSTLY GREETINGS!

HALLOWEEN IS A REAL TREAT

GHOSTLY GREETINGS!

HALLOWEEN IS A REAL TREAT

HAVE A
FANG-TASTIC
NIGHT

HAPPY HALLOWEEN!
TIME TO CARVE OUT THE PUMPKIN, BRING OUT THE CANDIES AND LET'S GET SUGAR HIGH

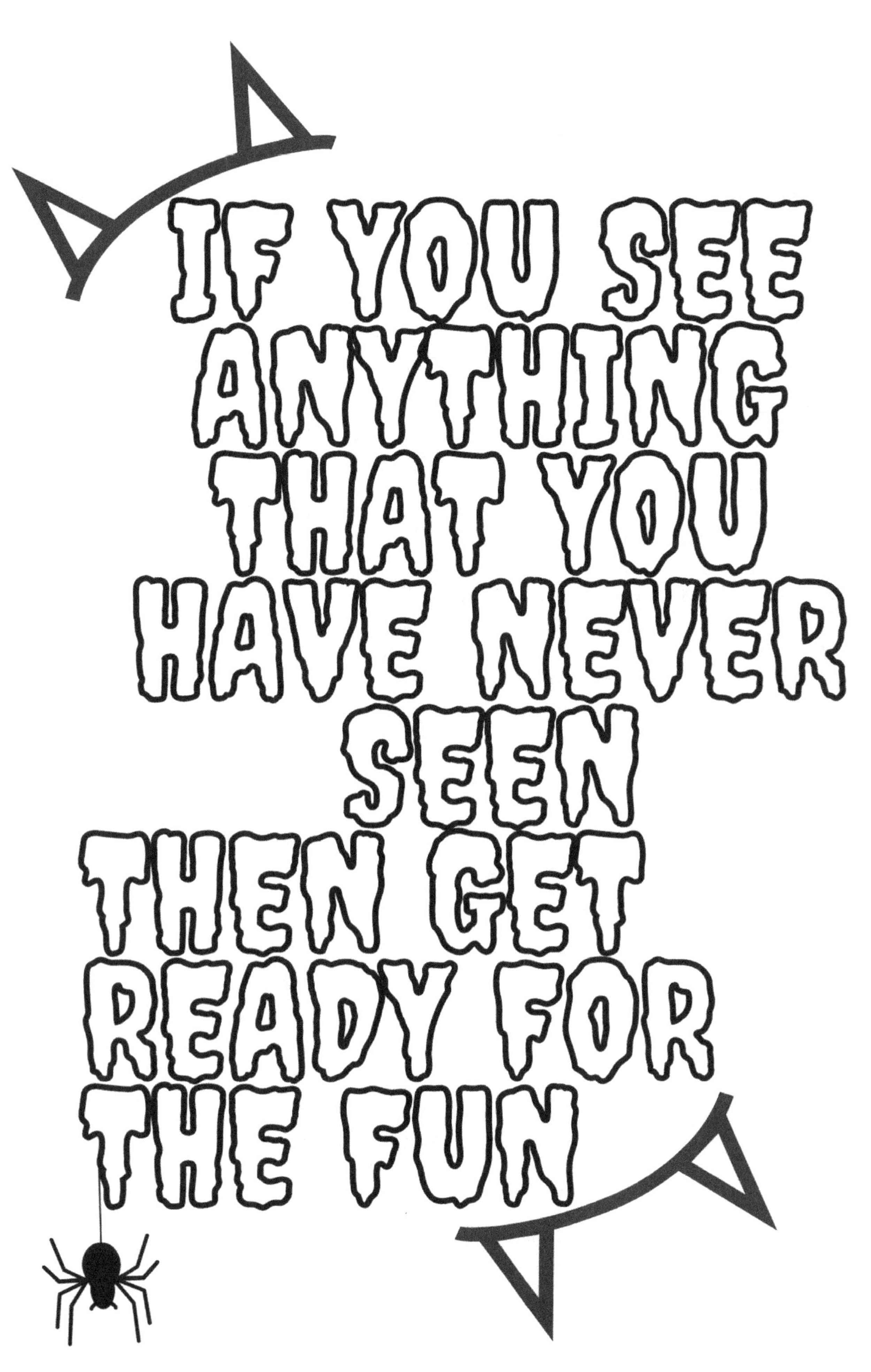

IF YOU SEE ANYTHING THAT YOU HAVE NEVER SEEN THEN GET READY FOR THE FUN

DON'T BE A
SCAREDY CAT

KEEP CALM
AND SCARE
ON.

EAT, DRINK, AND BE A MONSTER.

CUTEST PUMPKIN IN THE PATCH

IF YOU WANT A TASTY SWEET......BE SURE TO HOLLER TRICK OR TREAT!

MAY YOU SCARE MORE AND GET SCARED LESS ON THIS HALLOWEEN

THIS WITCH
CAN BE
BRIBED WITH
CHOCOLATE.

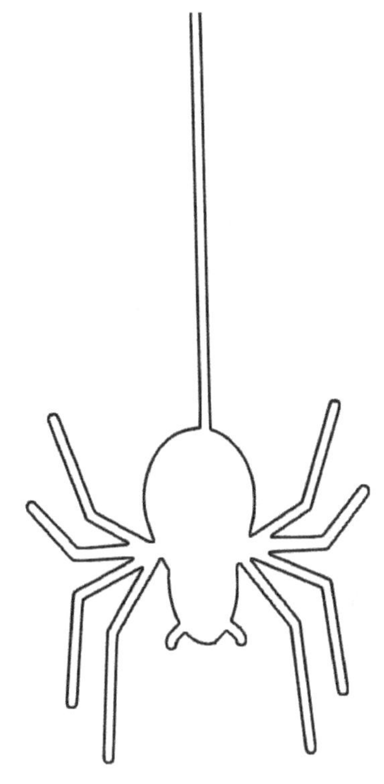

NO TRICKS, JUST TREATS!

SOMETHING WICKED THIS WAY COMES.

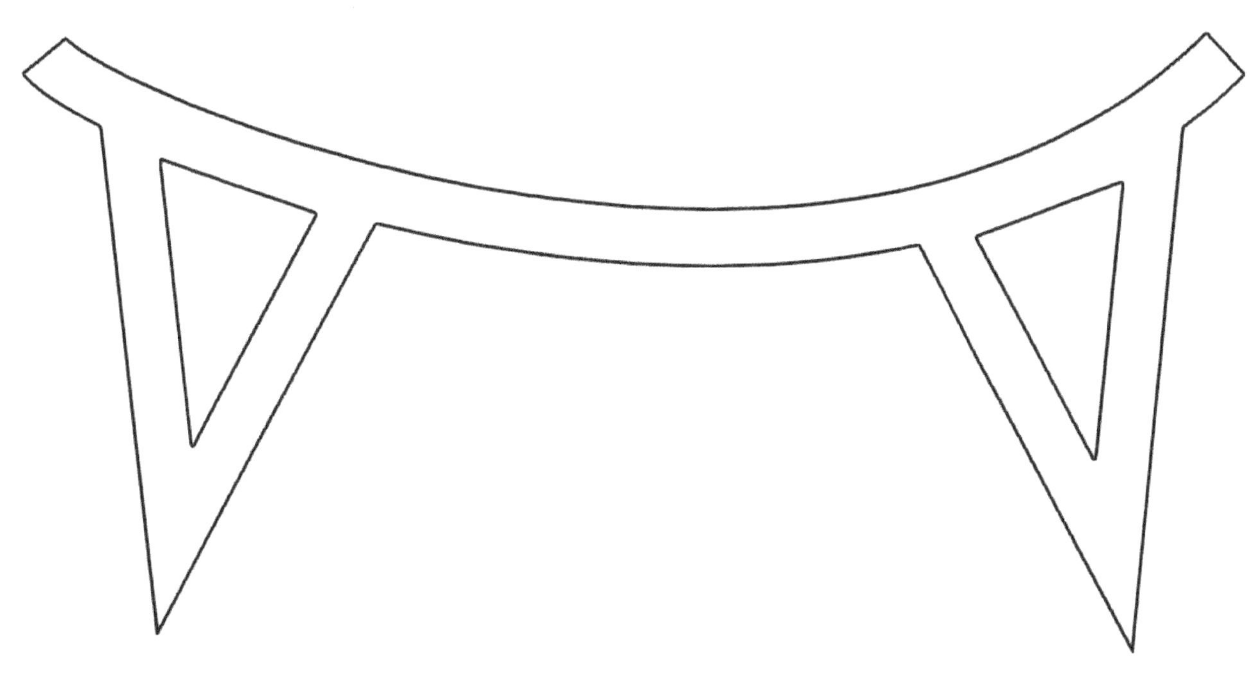
HAVE A
BOOTIFUL
HALLOWEEN

WITCHFUL THINKING.

HAVING A BOO-TIFUL NIGHT.
BOO!

THIS HALLOWEEN I'D LIKE TO TELL YOU A THING OR TWO, IT'S OKAY TO BE THE DEVIL, IT'S OKAY TO HAVE A TATTOO, IT'S OKAY TO BE AN ANGEL, IT'S OKAY TO TRICK OR TREAT TOO.

MISCHIEF MANAGED.

TOO CUTE TO SPOOK.

TOO GHOUL FOR SCHOOL.

IF YOU THINK YOU ARE BRAVE THEN ASK FOR THE TREAT AT A GRAVE.

GHOULS JUST WANNA HAVE FUN!

BOO FROM
THE CREW.

BRRR ...

IT'S COLD IN HERE.
THERE MUST BE
SOME SPIRITS IN
THE ATMOSPHERE!

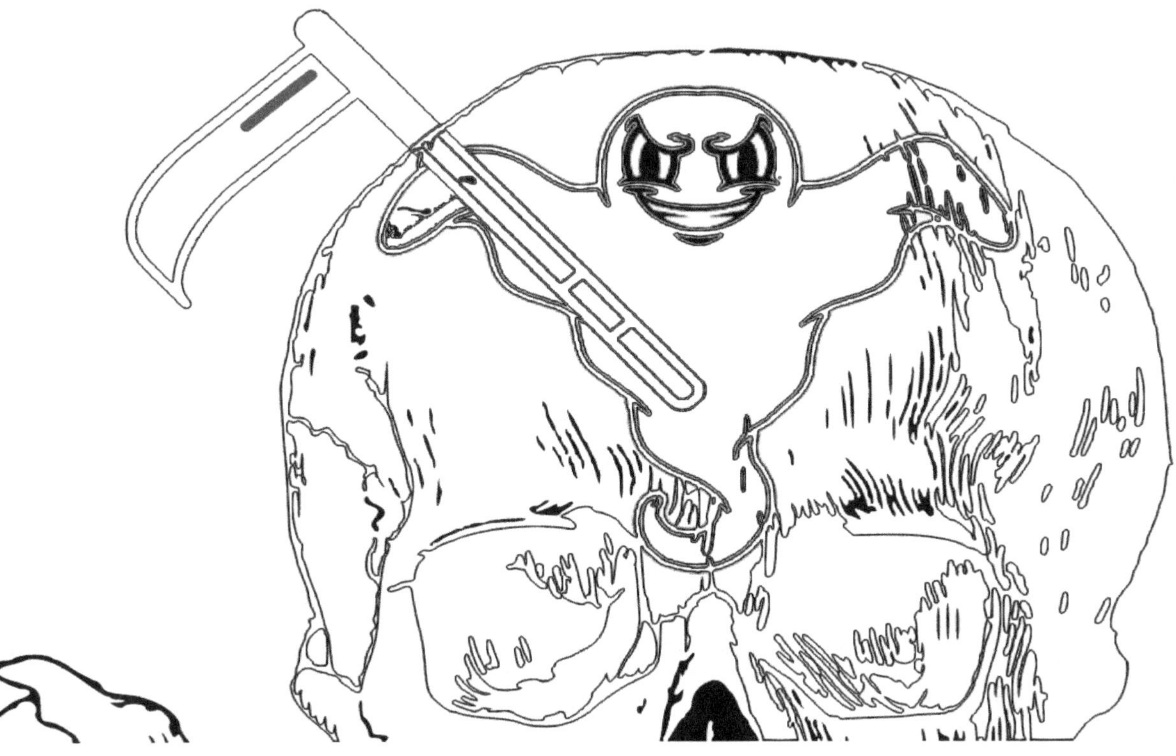

CREATURE FEATURE.

KEEP CALM AND
CARRY A WAND.

BUGS AND
HISSES.

BAD TO THE BONE.

I AM GUILTY OF
EATING
CANDY IN COLD
BLOOD

YOU'VE GOT
ME UNDER
YOUR SPELL.

HAPPY HOWL-OWEEN.

KEEP IT CREEPY!
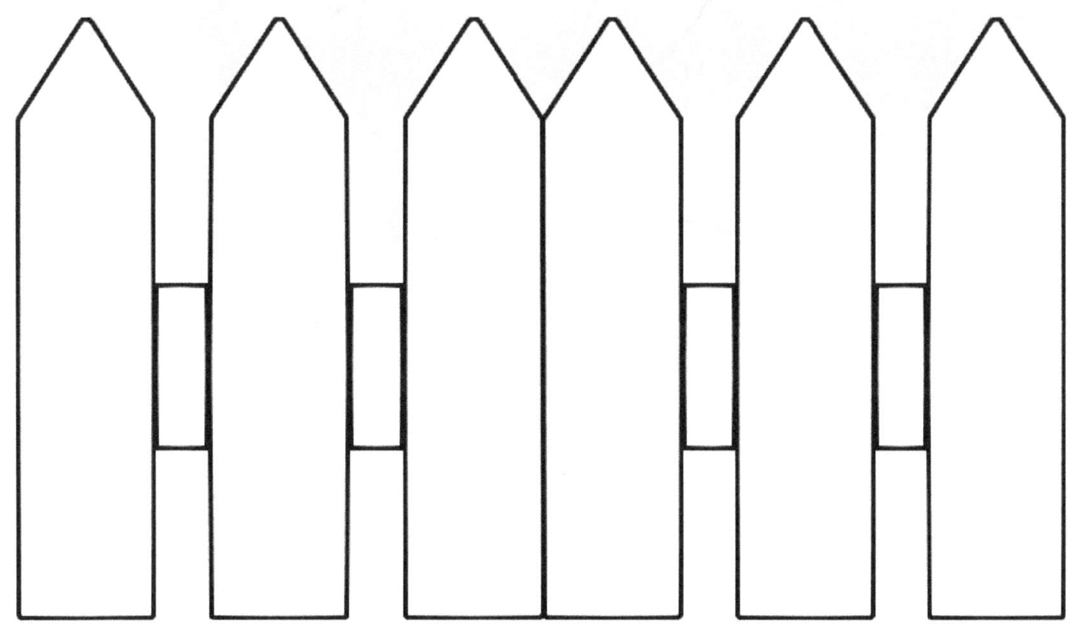

HAPPY HAIRY, HOWLING HALLOWEEN!

READY, SET, GHOUL!

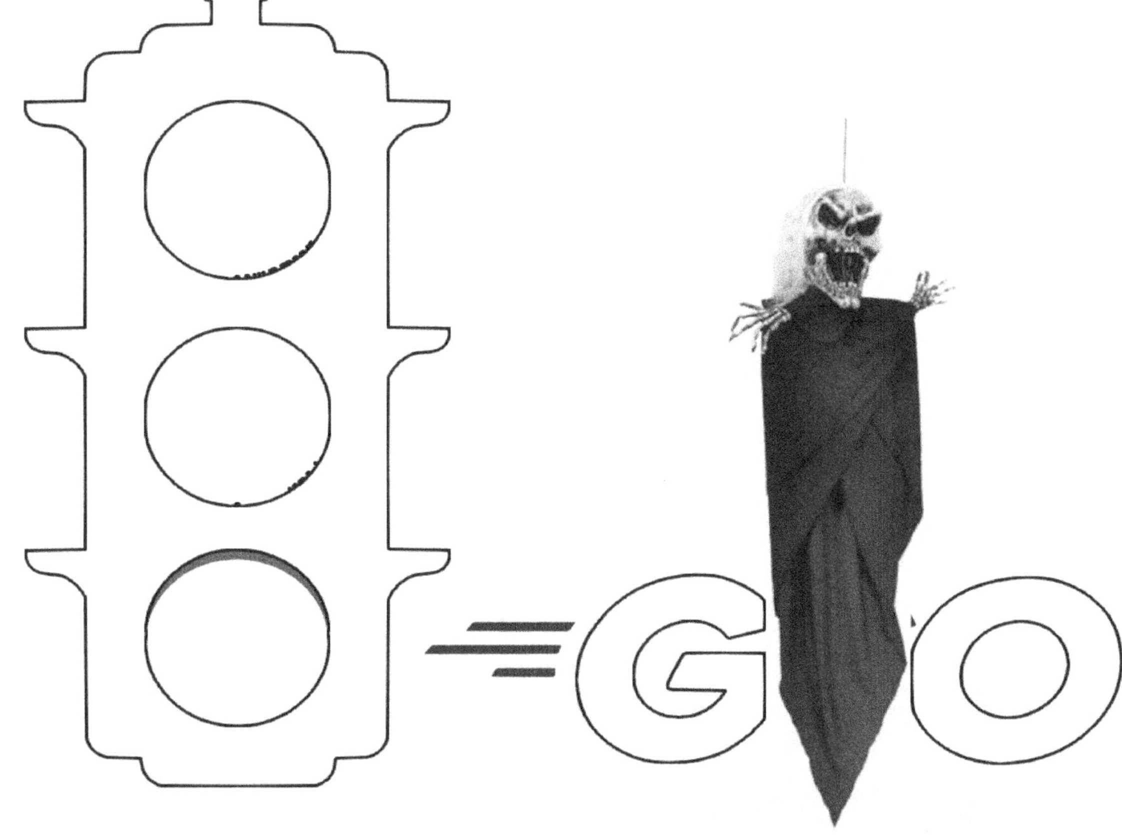

ABSOLUTELY
FA-BOO-LOUS.

KEEP CALM, TRICK OR TREAT AND CARRY ON.

I WAVE MY WAND AND PUT ON MY CAPE AND WISH YOU LOTS OF TREATS AND SUCCESS COMING YOUR WAY.

TRICK OR TREAT, BAGS OF
SWEETS, GHOSTS ARE
WALKING DOWN THE
STREET.

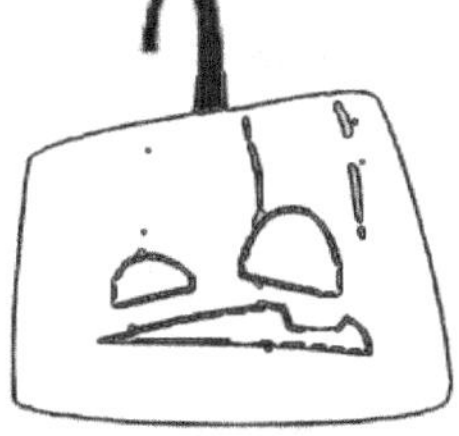

WHEN HALLOWEEN IS HERE THE MONSTERS APPEAR AND THE CANDIES DISAPPEAR.

EVERYTHING'S
BETTER WITH
A LITTLE
MAGIC.

THIS IS WHERE THE MAGIC HAPPENS.

HOPE ALL THE CANDIES DON'T GO TO WAIST.

HAPPY HALLOWEEN!

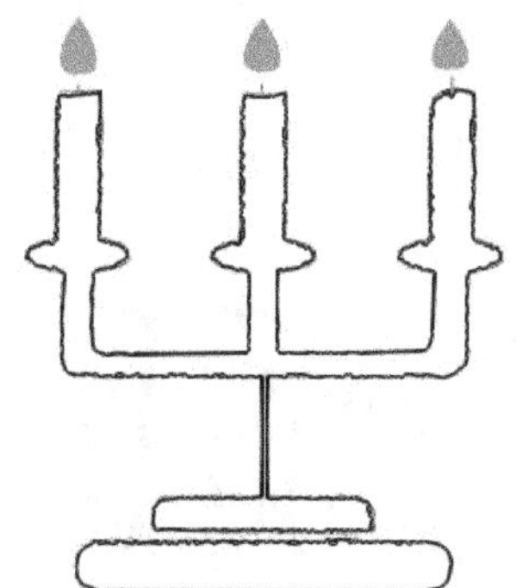

HAPPY HALLOWEEN TO
A COOL GHOUL.

MAY YOU HAVE A BAG FULL OF CANDY, BONES, BATS AND LOADS OF FUN. HAPPY HALLOWEEN!

I CAN BE MOODY BUT BE A LITTLE WITCH!

REESE'S IN PEACE.

HAVE A SPOOK-
TACULAR HALLO
WEEN!

A CANDY A DAY KEEPS THE MONSTERS AWAY.

A REAL WITCH IS NOTHING WITHOUT HER GHOUL FRIENDS.

THIS HALLOWEEN I'D LIKE TO TELL YOU A THING OR TWO, IT'S OKAY TO BE THE DEVIL, IT'S OKAY TO HAVE A TATTOO, IT'S OKAY TO BE AN ANGEL, IT'S OKAY TO TRICK OR TREAT TOO.

THIS LETTER IS SEALED WITH A VAMPIRE KISS AND BITE

HAVE A
GOOD HALLOWEEN NIGHT.
DON'T LET THE
BAD BATS BITE!

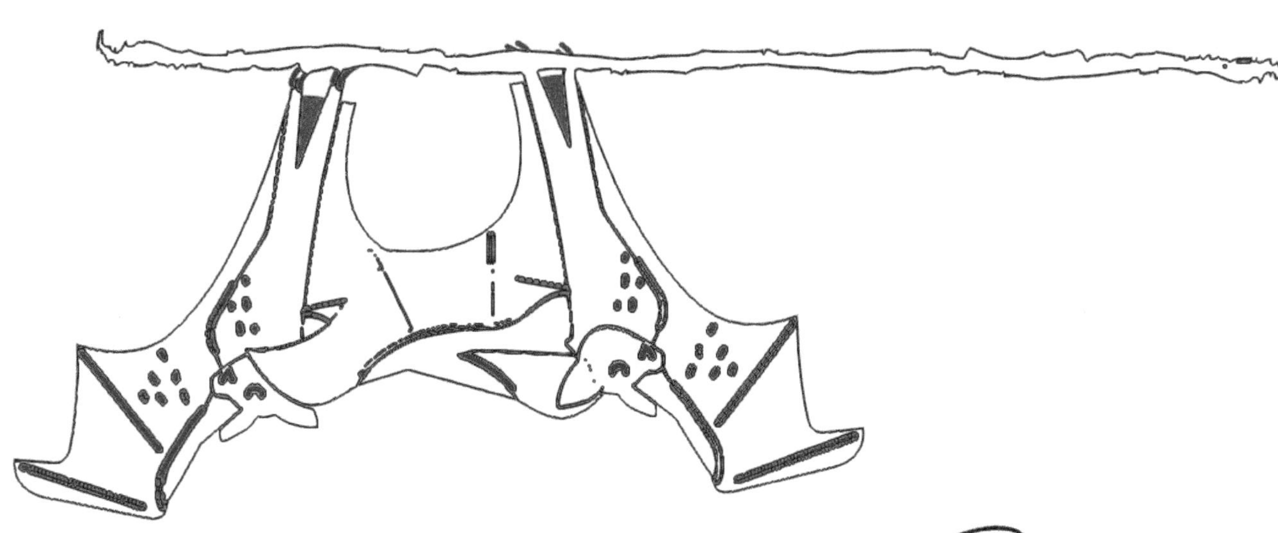

MAY THE
GHOST BE
WITH YOU.